# ESSAYS ON SOCIAL AND POLITICAL QUESTIONS

# ESSAYS ON SOCIAL AND POLITICAL QUESTIONS

BY

J. HOWARD WHITEHOUSE, M.P.

Cambridge

at the University Press

1913

# CAMBRIDGE
UNIVERSITY PRESS

University Printing House, Cambridge CB2 8BS, United Kingdom

Cambridge University Press is part of the University of Cambridge.

It furthers the University's mission by disseminating knowledge in the pursuit of education, learning and research at the highest international levels of excellence.

www.cambridge.org
Information on this title: www.cambridge.org/9781107456037

© Cambridge University Press 1913

First published 1913
First paperback edition 2014

*A catalogue record for this publication is available from the British Library*

ISBN 978-1-107-45603-7 Paperback

TO

MY FRIEND

NOEL BUXTON, M.P.

IN MEMORY OF ADVENTURES

AND EXPERIMENTS JOINTLY UNDERTAKEN

THIS BOOK IS AFFECTIONATELY DEDICATED

1 *December* 1913

I DESIRE to express my gratitude to the editors of *The Nineteenth Century* and *The Contemporary Review* for permission to reprint the articles which appeared in their respective pages.

J. H. W.

# CONTENTS

# BULGARIA AND SERVIA IN WAR: THE REVELATION OF NATIONALITY

# BULGARIA AND SERVIA IN WAR: THE REVELATION OF NATIONALITY[1]

IT is the desire of the writer to attempt some record of the revelation of the spirit of the Bulgarian and Servian peoples at this supreme crisis of their destiny. It is a difficult task for anyone to attempt from the outside to interpret that revelation, but perhaps it may not be wholly impossible for it to be, in part at least, appreciated by one who has had some exceptional opportunities for studying during the war time the attitude of these peoples, and the views and aims of their leaders.

It may be said with entire truth that the capitals of Bulgaria and Servia—Sofia and Belgrade—each epitomise at once the history and the character of the peoples whose centres of government they are. The cities of Sofia and Belgrade would be impressive even to the casual visitor in times of peace. They afford

[1] This essay originally appeared in the *Nineteenth Century* for January 1913. The subsequent war between the allies—a horrible interlude—does not I think interfere with the truth of the picture I attempted to draw, and I therefore issue the Essay unchanged.

an arresting contrast to the great European capitals.
They do not offer the pleasures, the refinements, the
luxuries, the vices, of the latter; they give us no
picture of great sections of the community passing
their days in idle amusements. Their buildings may
be primitive and crude, yet no man who had eyes to
see and ears to hear could doubt that he was in a city
of real men fighting for the real things of life. They
are cities of simple, hardy, strong people, building up
a national life amid incredibly difficult conditions, and
working out their destiny with patience and courage
never excelled. Such would be a true description of
these cities in times of peace. In this hour of war
they have not only the interest arising from the unique
history of their peoples, but they hold the observer
fascinated before the exhibition of a national spirit
which alone has made the supreme struggle possible.

It is difficult to express adequately and clearly the
subtle distinctions between the Bulgarian and the
Servian nations, springing from different stocks and
having very dissimilar histories, though strangely alike
in their tale of oppression by a common foe and their
partial liberation. In this time of war, when the
soldiers of each country are fighting side by side for
a common end and their statesmen are working in
active alliance, these differences tend to become much
more obscure to the observer, who first sees their
common aim, their common service, and their common
heroism, and it is my desire rather to present the unity
of the two peoples in their spirit and their aims than
to search minutely for the characteristics which divide

them. For these are chiefly matters of individual temperament, springing from racial differences.

The picture, therefore, that I seek to give of Bulgaria and Servia will attempt to present the essential harmony of which the war is but one revelation, and the object can perhaps best be attained by considering in turn the two cities of Sofia and Belgrade.

Sofia to-day presents the spectacle of an entirely united people. Here, at the brain of Bulgaria, is seen the courage of a people who are deliberately facing the most extreme forms alike of individual and of national suffering, not for greed, or revenge, or any unworthy object, but for the elemental things in life, for the right of their kindred to live, for the right of a civilised people to be emancipated from a barbarism and a tyranny which have brought upon them sufferings not exceeded in the history of the world. To be in Sofia to-day, when her people are engaged in this struggle, is a wonderful experience, filling the observer with joy and pride indeed, yet with great humility too. The attitude of the city is so simple, unaffected, so free from consciousness that their nation is doing one of the great things of history. The Bulgarians are un-demonstrative; their words are few; they have no gifts of rhetoric; they have no feeling for pageants. Yet Sofia to-day is the most wonderful of all pageants —a nation in sacrifice.

The first fact which is realised beyond the possibility of doubt or misgiving is the national character of the movement which has produced the present position. No national struggle has ever been of a more democratic nature, and the heroism of the soldiers finds its fitting complement in the self-sacrifice and devotion shown in every section of the nation, but, in a pre-eminent degree, by her women.

There are not many men in Sofia to-day: those who are able to be there are at the war. A large part of the life of the city is carried on by the women, just as in the fields throughout the country women and children have taken the place of the men, and the women have shown themselves to be not less heroic than the men. The wounded, after sufferings on the journey which cannot be described, are, as far as possible, ultimately brought to Sofia, and are sheltered in the various public buildings throughout the city. The women of Sofia, including those of the highest rank, from early morning until late at night spend their days nursing in these hospitals. It is a service entered upon without distinction of any kind. Their work is beyond all praise. It is done with courage and joy and wholehearted devotion, all private interests being placed on one side. Their spirit is the same as that of their husbands and brothers and sons in the trenches at the front.

Perhaps the services at the Cathedral are an even more wonderful manifestation of the national spirit. Let me recall one memorable service at which I was present. It was at the moment of the Armistice, and was held in the old Cathedral. The Bulgarian Church possesses the doctrine and forms of the Greek Orthodox Church, though it is not a branch of that Church. It is a secessionist Church, and is entirely self-governing and national.   On the occasion I am recalling there was a typical Bulgarian congregation.   No seats are provided in the Cathedral, and the crowded congregation stood motionless for two hours.   There were not many young men to be counted: they were elsewhere.   There were a great number of women, some old, some young, many in the simple and distinctive peasant dress of the country, and there were many children.   There were some soldiers freshly discharged from the hospitals, and about to return to the front; there were a number of old men.   The Government had issued an edict that the names of none of the men who were wounded or killed should be published, and this order was being rigidly adhered to in Bulgaria. Its object was to prevent private grief from interfering with the discharge of public duty, for the women, and even the children of the nation, were wanted for other things than household duties.   In the congregation, therefore, at the service I speak of, there would be very few indeed who had not near relatives at the front, of whose fate they were ignorant.   Yet, in spite of the overwhelming personal anxiety which must have been felt, the feeling was irresistible that this was a gathering of people conscious of national victory.   It was not that there was not intense gravity, and even much sorrow; indeed, when one saw the faces of many of the women as they knelt before the pictures of the Virgin, the irresistible force of Shakespeare's lines was realised :

> Such eyes the widows in Corioli wear,
> And mothers that lack sons.

But it was borne upon one that the note of personal grief was merged in the greater note of common service and sacrifice. The service itself was a tribute to the simplicity of the nation. Though it was marked in parts by stately ritual, and was assisted by music of exquisite beauty, the note of homeliness was never lost. The priests, indeed, were clothed in gorgeous vestments, but their acolytes were little boys clothed in their simple dress of the working world. Later these lads collected the offertory, and, with curious dignity and grace, threaded their way through the crowded ranks of the congregation. The note of homeliness was again struck at the end of the service, when not only the men and the women, but also the little children, pressed forward to receive the wine and the bread which had been blessed during the service, or to have the holy oil placed upon their lips. You were at a family gathering, sharing a common task and a common faith.

It was interesting to contrast such a congregation with the gatherings one remembered at home during the South African War. There were essential differences, perhaps most noticeable in the matter of dress; for, although some of the older women wore black, there was no attempt on the part of the congregation generally to make any alteration in the colours and the arrangement of their usual dress. The simplicity, the earnestness, the piety, the heroism of the service were the simplicity, the earnestness, the piety, the heroism of the battlefield.

The next fundamental thing which is realised by

the traveller in Bulgaria is that the feats of arms performed by the Bulgarians in the field are not more wonderful than the feats which have been performed by the Bulgarians in time of peace. When one is in Sofia, it seems almost incredible that a little more than thirty years ago the town was under Turkish domination, misgoverned and squalid. This well-ordered town, built between two ranges of mountains, with a great and vigorous life, the centre of a healthy people, arduously gaining their living for the most part by the cultivation of the soil, is in itself the justification of the independence of her nation—of her past claims, her present endeavours. The more detailed the examination into the social fabric built up in these few short years, the more wonderful it appears. The prosperity of the peasants, the security and happiness of life in the villages and districts formerly devastated by the Turk; the high statesmanship at the seat of government, which, whilst securing the defence of the nation, has promoted its brilliant industrial success, and has shown a wisdom and resourcefulness second to that of no European Power; the adoption of a system of popular education, upon which is spent a greater proportion of the national resources than is spent, for instance, in Great Britain—these are at once the expression of the national spirit and its triumphant vindication.

Perhaps the writer may be forgiven if he attempts further to illustrate what he has endeavoured to describe of the spirit of Bulgaria by a brief reference to conversations he had with the Prime Minister and

other Ministers in Sofia. It would be a poor return
for their kindness to assume for a moment the position
of interpreting their views on the immediate questions
raised by the war and the conferences now proceeding.
But I may, without, I hope, being guilty of any breach
of hospitality, attempt in a word to set forth my own
impression of the manner in which King Ferdinand's
Ministers embody and reflect the national spirit.

I can well imagine visitors from the great capitals
of the world feeling a tendency to smile at the simplicity of the machinery of government in Bulgaria—the
simple residences of Ministers and officers of State,
the almost peasant simplicity of the Government
offices, the absence of all ostentation and ceremonial.
These things are all typical of the splendid simplicity
of the Bulgar spirit. But simplicity does not mean
stupidity, and the rulers of Bulgaria are worthy of
their task. In all that I heard and learnt from the
Prime Minister I saw the reflection of the soul of the
nation : its bravery and its fortitude. What impressed
me more than anything, if I may without impertinence
say so, was the singular nobility of spirit shown in the
attitude of the head of the Government towards the
Turk. In the hour of victory there was no note of
exultation. There was gentleness and humility. And
there was the vision of the statesman looking to a new
dawn across the hilltops of time.

At the moment of which I write, the head of the
Bulgarian Government was grappling with a combina-
tion of problems unique in the history of statesmanship.
What these were is a matter of public knowledge, but

to be appreciated they should be set forth. They included (*a*) the war itself, with the countless daily questions it involved for the constant consideration of the Government; (*b*) the alliance between the Balkan nations, with the special problems inseparable from it; (*c*) the negotiation of the armistice with the Turks; (*d*) the relations with the Great Powers; (*e*) the conditions of permanent peace, and the instructions to the delegates to the Peace Conference; (*f*) the establishment of civil government in the captured territory. The list is not exhaustive, but it is sufficient! Each of these matters demanded from the head of the Government the utmost resources of statesmanship, and the demand was met. All who met the Prime Minister during these days could not fail to be impressed with his consummate ability. It was united to a simple and unaffected directness of expression which exhibited the harmony of the nation; for the Premier's views were his country's views, and the policy pursued by the Government was understood and approved by the people. The just simplicity of that policy succeeded, where subtle balancings and diplomatic manœuvrings would have failed.

The attitude of the Government, calm and dauntless before difficulties as great as any nation ever faced, represented, too, that of the Sobranye, which re-assembled after the armistice was concluded, and without demonstration, excitement, or passion, either by their own members or the general public, proceeded to consider the immediate financial and administrative questions which awaited them. A further evidence of the solidarity of the nation was seen in the gift by the whole of the civil servants of two-thirds of their salaries, as a contribution towards the cost of the war.

Belgrade presents, as a city, a great contrast to Sofia; it is cruder; it gives the not unjust impression that its people are not so far advanced in the gentler arts of life. The application of the resources of modern science to the needs of everyday life has not been carried so far as at Sofia. There is not quite the same social note. The first impression the traveller receives is that he is in the centre of a nation of peasants, who have been too hard at work struggling for existence to have had time for the gentler amenities of life; but the attitude of the people as a community is wonderfully similar to the attitude of the sister nation. There is the same unity of purpose, the same intense patriotism (though perhaps more demonstratively expressed); there is, of course, the same problem of the conflict with the historic forces of barbarism. There is, too, the realisation of the great part their people have played in history. They are conscious of the splendid heritage which reaches them from far-distant days.

In some respects, the present position achieved by Servia is even more wonderful than that of Bulgaria; because Servia has not only had to liberate herself from the Turk, but has had to consolidate her nation and build up its economic welfare, with a hostile Power on her northern frontier, making her to a great extent an economic prisoner.

The strain upon the Servian people during the present war has been acute, for, whilst her armies in the field have been shedding their blood in driving back the Turk, they have had the added strain of fearing that at any moment a yet greater conflict might be upon them by the interposition of Austria; yet there has been no panic, no hesitancy, no feverish alteration of plans or balancing of odds. Servia has done the work to hand, and for the rest has trusted to the national spirit and to the justice of her cause and claims.

Its capital is a town of grim realities. At its very doors the great Austrian army is massing itself. Most of her sons are away at the front, save only those who have returned to fill the hospitals dotted all over the town.

Though we are now in a different nation, sharing not even a common language with Bulgaria, the essential unity in spirit of the two nations is manifest. The Servian women are showing the same resourcefulness and self-sacrifice as in Bulgaria. There is the same consolidation through every section of the nation. I had some striking proofs of what Servian nationality means to the individual Serb. At the hotel at which I was staying three of the waiters were Serbs who had just returned to Belgrade after some years' absence. Two of them held profitable posts in London; the other owned a thriving business in New York. These three men had voluntarily and without summons put aside their work and hastened to Servia. Arriving there, they had then reported themselves, and whilst waiting to be sent with the second reserve to the front, had taken posts as waiters, and quietly awaited orders.

I was further enabled by conversation with many people, including some of very humble rank, to realise the breadth of view of the Servian. The humblest Serb understood real politics. He was not taking part in a movement in which he was simply a tool. He had knowledge of what the movement meant to him and to his nation. It was interesting to see how he viewed the circumstances attending the violent change in the monarchy which placed the present King upon the throne. That incident, shocking as he admits it to have been, brought to an end a condition of things to him much more shocking. He sees in it a violent but unavoidable step in the emancipation and development of his people. He tolerates outside criticism, and replies to it in the spirit of one feeling that to know all is to forgive all. I am not seeking to justify or to condemn this attitude, but to record it.

The appearance of Belgrade during the war is in itself a symptom of the temperamental differences between the Bulgar and the Serb. Here in Belgrade there is more direct expression. Even the street costers display the national colours over their stalls ; but more significant is the exhibition at various places in the town of large oil paintings, showing with horrible realism some of the barbarities practised by the Turks upon their subjects and prisoners.

It must not, however, be assumed that the graces of life are neglected by the Serb. I had the opportunity of observing the courtesy and consideration with which the Turkish officers who were prisoners in Belgrade were treated. The relations which the Servian officers attempted to establish with them maintained the highest traditions of chivalry.

And in this city, which, if subjected to the valueless test of physical comparison with the great capitals of the world, appears so crude and rough, there is much to cause searchings of heart to the visitor. The whining beggar of our cities is not to be seen in Belgrade, and though perhaps the more finished graces of life are not to be found, there are civility and kindness everywhere. It would even seem that the roughness of the climate has brought its own amenities into the daily lives of the people, for the boys selling newspapers in the streets carry their papers in neat portfolios, are clean to look at, and never enter a shop or public room without carefully wiping their shoes and generally removing their caps.

Some mention should be made of the passionate affection which is felt both in Servia and Bulgaria for Britain. Notwithstanding some historic failures on our part, we are still in their eyes their traditional friends. For we are the countrymen of Gladstone, the reverence for whom is to-day as great as when he thundered against their enemies and oppressors ; and in the work of the Balkan Committee they see the spirit of Gladstone animating his nation to-day. The affection of a nation is not a treasure to be lightly held. In this case it will, I believe, increase rather than diminish, but it is well that we should realise its existence and its strength, and the possibilities which

lie therein.   One practical suggestion I would venture
to make in this connexion—the immediate organisation of facilities for giving a number of Bulgarian and
Servian students the opportunity of education in
England.

It has not been my purpose, except incidentally, to
speak of the war itself, the brilliance of its tactics, and
the gallantry of the troops.   These are now matters of
world knowledge.   But one thing should be said.   It
may with justice be urged that this war was not only
justifiable, but, if such a term could ever be used of
war, was almost ideal in its justice.   It may be so.
But no one who faintly realises what the war has cost
these great peoples in suffering and sorrow, not to
speak of material waste, can assent to such a view without qualification.   The war may indeed be justifiable:
it may even be ideal.   But the justice and the idealism
are the possessions of the peoples who are fighting for
life itself.   And the Powers of Europe, which might
have achieved the cause of the Allies without imposing
on them this supreme trial, must not be allowed to
forget their direct responsibility.

# BRITAIN AND GERMANY

# BRITAIN AND GERMANY[1]

THE immediate crisis between the two countries has passed: misunderstanding, suspicion, ignorance, these remain, with a new and more intense irritation, and the relations between the two countries are more seriously strained than at any period in the past. Each side may not unreasonably urge some justification for the present feeling. We have been angered and alarmed by the violence and brusqueness of the Agadir method, and by flamboyant and provocative speech. The Germans are aggrieved at what they feel to be the entire misunderstanding of their aims shown in the speeches of statesmen here, and at the check given to what they feel to be legitimate enterprises. Each has reason to complain of the other's Press, its truculent sensationalism and the partiality of ignorant prejudice.

## The Present Position

The tragedy behind the present manifestations of feeling is that they do not represent the real spirit of either nation. In Germany opinion is led by a small official group, and the leading newspapers, to an extent

[1] *Nineteenth Century*, November 1911.

unknown in this country, are inspired and guided by this group. The view that we get, therefore, of German public opinion is not necessarily representative of the nation. Even to-day the feeling in Germany towards this country is vitally different from that reflected in her and our journals. There is a small governing caste which is intensely irritated and suspicious, and which regards our motives and conduct in much the same light as we regard theirs. There is also a considerable section of the military and naval classes which would frankly welcome an outbreak of hostilities. But behind these adverse influences there is to be found a vast public opinion seldom reaching this land, but which is more representative of the soul of the German people than the engineered agitation which chiefly reaches us. The organised forces of social democracy, in which the approaching elections will, it is believed, show a striking increase, however disturbing in the domestic life of Germany, stand in international life for methods of understanding and peace. The vast majority of the middle classes desire friendship with this country, and were the Reichstag not so powerless to influence foreign policy, this desire would be more clearly reflected. The hostility which exists, and it would be idle to deny that there is much, is due to the belief in the same kind of bogies which do service in this country—fear that our fleet is intended for their destruction, and that between the two countries there are irreconcilable differences. There are no definite issues. So far as its people is concerned, each country follows an unknown path upon

an unknown quest, with the result that two great
nations are in angry antagonism, though their interests
do not necessarily clash.

It has been interesting to study in Germany the
effect which has been produced by the Chancellor of
the Exchequer's speech to the bankers. Everywhere
it has made a profound impression, and it has given
alarm and pain in the circles most favourable to Britain
and most active for friendship. This effect is here
recorded, not in order to criticise the Chancellor of the
Exchequer, who spoke for the Government, and whose
words were endorsed by both political parties, but in
order that its explanation may point a moral. The
Chancellor has a great international reputation, and
a large section of the German people look with
admiration on his advocacy of schemes of social
reform, which appeal alike to their social and intellectual
sympathies, and some of which they feel their own
example has influenced. Hence, just as Mr Gladstone,
in some aspects of his public work—*e.g.* his passionate
sympathy for oppressed nationalities—was regarded in
other countries as one whose work was not confined to
his own people, but appealed to the sympathy of sister
nations, so the Chancellor of the Exchequer, in some
aspects of his work as a British statesman, has made
a similar appeal to the sympathy of a not inconsiderable
section of the German people, and the pain which has
been shown at his recent speech in the less political
circles of Germany is the measure of their disappoint-
ment at realising how deep must be the British distrust
of German aims when they are so misunderstood by

one who stood to them in this special position. Let there be further remembered in justification of this feeling the entirely sincere belief held in many German circles favourable to Britain that their Government from the first had no intention or desire to remain at Agadir.

The writer has had the opportunity in Germany of hearing the views of leading members of different parties in the Reichstag, the editors of some of the greater papers, the heads of the Churches, representative bankers and business men, and social experts and writers.

From all these representatives of widely differing phases of social life and thought came the same revealing and consistent note, a passionate feeling that their country's desires and ideals were vitally misunderstood by Britain, and that Britain's attitude was based upon that misunderstanding. When we realise here how sincerely this belief is held throughout the German nation, we shall have taken a considerable step in the right direction.

### The Policy of Britain

A brief reference must be made to the policy of recent British Governments with regard to Germany. Time slowly reveals that which diplomacy hides, and there is some justification for thinking that the policy of Britain has been based upon suspicion and fear. It has seen in the German shipbuilding programme a menace to our navy. It has perhaps looked upon the aspirations of a progressive and expanding nation as ideals which can only be realised at the expense of our own colonies or other vital interests. It seeks safety by keeping ahead in the race of armaments, and by drawing within the bond of friendly treaty other nations which share our feelings.

Is this policy an adequate one? Where does it lead us? An unchecked race in armaments must eventually reach a limit. Before that limit is reached the growing anger of each nation must issue in war. If it were not so supremely tragic there would be both pathos and comedy in the belief so strongly held that a war, even if successful, would benefit this country. We do not speak of the horror which even the thought of such a strife must inspire; of its cost in sorrow, of the drainage of wealth greater than that which may be counted in values of gold. But these things would all be vain. The destruction of the German fleet, could that be accomplished, would not defeat a nation in all the vigour of its youth. Rivalry and enmity would not be checked. Lasting peace and the reduction of armaments would be as distant in the hour of victory as in the hour of defeat.

The criticism, then, which must be made of our policy with regard to Germany is that it is inadequate. We would substitute for our present negative attitude a constructive policy based upon the frank recognition of the community of interests between the two nations, recognising the natural desire of Germany to have play for legitimate national aspirations. It should be our aim not only to seek harmonious co-operation with Germany, but also to use our influence with France in such a way as to make friendly relations between France and Germany a matter of practical statesmanship. The tradition of the Concert of Europe might at last become a living reality.

Is it merely the expression of an impossible dream to say that war to-day, so far as the great civilised Powers are concerned, should be employed if at all only in defence of a common civilisation ? It may be that the day will dawn more speedily than we think, when the dissensions in the European Courts will be vital weaknesses in the presence of a common danger now hidden or but dimly perceived.

### *Towards a Constructive Policy*

We pass, then, to the consideration of definite proposals for the attainment of lasting peace. Most of them are addressed primarily to members of the Houses of Parliament, for on their influence the immediate future depends.

(1) The solution of the existing situation is not to be found by a reduction of the Naval Estimates of this country, as an isolated act of policy, and to urge this at the moment is waste of effort. Reduction must be mutual, but can only follow an understanding, and before an understanding is possible a new atmosphere has to be created in both countries.

(2) The present system under which Parliament is kept without knowledge of foreign policy, and without the opportunity of exercising influence, should be modified. The writer does not forget that a large part of the details of negotiations with foreign

countries must necessarily be secret in the future as in the past; but this is not to say that the representatives of the nation are to be allowed to have no voice even in the discussion of the broad principles of our foreign policy, or that we are to be brought to the verge of war without any influence having had play outside a small circle of diplomatists.

How to secure this discussion and influence without prejudice to national interests is a serious problem. We are, however, in this country under a more than usually secret system so far as relations with other countries are concerned. The writer would like further consideration to be given to the possibility of a Foreign Relations Committee. There is at least this immediate argument to be used in its favour, that the wider the circle which shapes foreign policy, the more representative of the nation is it likely to be. It is a curious testimony to the present powerlessness of Parliament in foreign affairs that even to-day we have no knowledge of the nature of the existing treaty with France, its duration, its military or other responsibilities. Ought this knowledge any longer to be withheld?

(3) The British Government, with entire sincerity, has from time to time expressed its willingness to come to an arrangement with Germany on the basis of a mutual limitation of shipbuilding. The fact that this suggestion has not been accepted by Germany is not a sufficient reason for going no further. The resources of the Government are not exhausted by a proposal of that nature, and other means should be tried to reach the desired end.

Thus, for instance, there might be a special mission to Berlin. The choice of the man to represent us could not be too carefully made, but happily there is more than one fitted for this high duty. For ourselves we should be content if the choice fell upon Lord Haldane, who both by temperament and knowledge is singularly fitted for a duty demanding the highest powers of statesmanship. Such a mission would review the whole field of controversy, present or potential, between the two countries, and would seek not only the adjustment of present differences, but the formulating of a policy with reference to those subjects and countries which will clearly become matters of controversy in the future.

(4) There is an urgent need that each nation should have the knowledge of the other which alone can banish the cruder forms of prejudice in each country. At the Church Congress a large audience was deeply impressed by the view of Germany given by Sir Frank Lascelles, and greatly moved by his wise words on behalf of a friendship which he, with a unique experience, believed to be possible. Equally profound was the impression made by Lord Haldane's review of the history of modern Germany at the Oxford Summer Meeting. In both cases knowledge was substituted for ignorance, hope for fear. A prop was removed from the throne of the sensational Press. Similarly, let the two peoples obtain knowledge of each other. One step towards this would be for an exchange of visits between a representative number of members of the two Parliaments. We should like to begin by

having members of the Reichstag here as the guests
of Parliament, and letting them have the opportunity
not only to state with frankness their own views, but
also to hear the views of our own members.    But
apart from this it would be a great step gained to have
established direct personal relationships between the
members of the two Parliaments.

(5) It is difficult to make any definite proposal to
mitigate the evil caused by a section of the Press in
each country, and by the less-scrupulous foreign correspondents.    But something more might be done by
the greater papers not only to preserve the public from
vicious fictions, but also in taking a more active part
for the cause of friendship by giving a fuller picture of
German life, German thought, and German character,
realising that merely to print cabled extracts from
inspired or subsidised papers abroad is not to reach
any true appreciation or knowledge of the German
nation.    A word of protest may also be recorded here
against a practice which has caused great mischief in
Germany, the printing in certain weekly papers here
of cheap and lurid stories of invasion either of or by
this country.

(6) Believing with the late Ambassador to Germany
that friendly relations between the two nations are not
only possible but reasonable, we would ultimately
desire that an appeal be made to as representative
a body of public opinion in each country as is possible.
We would precede this appeal by the constructive
measures roughly outlined above, but ultimately the
policy approved by this nation should be made as clear

to the people of Germany as to our own. The prelude to this would be its clear definition on the floor of the House of Commons. It would not be a small achievement to have formulated a policy, the result of patient mission and of negotiation, which we could submit openly, if need be, for the judgment of the nations concerned. We are strong enough to do this.

The situation, though dark and threatening, is not without hope. Political memories are not so short as to forget that even worse relations existed with France not long ago, and with Russia before France. Patience, moderation, sincerity, will point the way of peace, and cause the present black cloud to recede perhaps for ever from our view.

# FOREIGN POLICY

# FOREIGN POLICY[1]

THE most inexperienced Member of this House
could not rise to speak on some of the aspects of the
questions which have arisen in the course of this
Debate without a feeling of great responsibility.
There is one school of writers and publicists who,
whilst with entire freedom giving expression to their
own warlike views, always urge that it is an embarrass-
ment to the Government of the day if we seek to
examine the principles which have inspired our relations with other countries—a school of writers who do
not hesitate themselves to give expression to views
which are repugnant to very many of us. In connexion
with this question of responsibility, I desire to say this,
that to those people the proper time for considering
principles of foreign policy never does arise, and
although I am conscious of the responsibility attaching

[1] A speech delivered in the House of Commons, December 14,
1911. The author asks for the forbearance of his readers for
including a Parliamentary speech in a volume of essays. It is
however complementary to the previous paper on Britain and
Germany. The occasion of the debate in the House of Commons
was a discussion on the causes of the crisis with Germany during
the previous summer.

to every word which is spoken in this House, yet I also rise to speak with confidence, because I desire only to appeal to principles of international co-operation and understanding. Therefore nothing that I can say could embarrass any party or any persons, except those who are hostile to such principles.

I think that the plea of secrecy and the plea of reserve in regard to foreign affairs is carried too far. I was struck by the speech that was delivered at an earlier period of this sitting by the hon. Member for Rugby (Mr Baird). I regret that he is not in his place. So far as I understood his remarks, he seems to consider that foreign policy is a matter of so much difficulty and delicacy that none but the professional diplomatists could grapple with it. I remember that a little time ago the same hon. Member went so far as to criticise the present Under-Secretary to the Board of Trade[1], who was then sitting on these Back Benches, because he had ventured to speak upon a subject of which he was a master, the subject of our policy in Egypt. I was at some loss to understand the attitude taken by the hon. Member for Rugby both to-day and on the former occasion until I remembered that the hon. Member was himself once attached to one of our Embassies. Therefore I take it—I speak without any desire of giving offence—that he spoke with the reserve proper to the expert who felt what a pity it was that the House of Commons should venture to express an opinion in matters which were only the business of the expert. I am glad to feel from the

[1] Mr J. M. Robertson.

great majority of the speeches that have been delivered to-night that the House generally does not take that view, and I am myself glad of the opportunity to inquire into the causes of the strained relations which have so long unhappily existed between this country and Germany, relations so strained that there has grown up a school of thought in this country which has publicly, on many occasions, proclaimed that war between the two countries is sooner or later inevitable.

I do not believe in this inevitable war. I remember that before this language was used with regard to Germany, the same kind of language was held with regard to other countries. If the House will pardon a personal reminiscence, one of the earliest recollections I have as a small schoolboy of one of my masters is the fact that he used to tell us, day after day, that we were on the brink of war with Russia, and that the sooner it came the better, because Russia was getting stronger every day. He used to make our blood curdle by reminding us that no sooner in this inevitable war had we defeated one huge battalion than another would be ready to take its place. I come to more recent years. I want to ask this House to remember the kind of relations which existed between this country and France. I hasten to say that in referring to the policy then urged with regard to France and the relations which then existed I am only filled with joy to think that happy relations exist to-day. It will be seen later that I in no way intend to belittle the friendly relations which now exist; indeed, if such were my aim, I should not choose this day to express it, when we all feel deeply the splendid heroism shown by the French sailors on behalf of our own people. But I want the House to remember the kind of feeling that did exist between this country and France for the decade previous to the French Agreement. I will not quote the more sensational Press of that time, but I want to show the public feeling that existed and the official feeling that existed by referring very briefly to the words of *The Times* during that period. I take, for instance, this extract. In January, 1896, *The Times* wrote :

"It is, unfortunately, the fact that there exists between ourselves and our French neighbours a considerable number of differences; the history, the traditions and the sentiments of the two peoples make them, to a great extent, inevitable."

And this is the theme recurring in almost every issue of the paper at times. We have frequently fierce protests being made against any curtailment of our own shipbuilding policy in view of the closeness of the French nation. In November, 1898, *The Times* wrote :

"We are not ignorant that preparations, both naval and military, are going on in France. We prefer to draw our own inference, and the inference from the silence and preparations of the French Government is that we ought to be prepared for whatever can happen."

But more than this, whilst these attacks were going on towards France, other sentiments were again being expressed with regard to Germany. I quote, for instance, this extract from *The Times* of November 18th, 1898, which was with special reference to a speech which had been delivered by the right hon. gentleman (Mr Joseph Chamberlain), whose absence from this House we all deplore:

"Another idea, of which Mr Chamberlain has been the apostle, is that in spite of keen commercial rivalry and of differences of national temper, fundamental interests and general similarity of aim and ideals ought to place England and Germany side by side in the secular movement of humanity. It is satisfactory to note that the German Press begins to acknowledge that there is something in this ideal. As a matter of fact, we have no standing disputes with Germany, nor is there any reason why the interests of the two countries should clash with Europe."

Then there is this significant passage:

"In the Colonial field we have not to complain of a policy of pin-pricks on the part of Germany, whose policy is always more positive and more obviously based upon the legitimate pursuit of solid interests than that of France. We want a measure of masculine friendship based upon mutual respect and proceeding upon the lines of mutual interest and community of aims."

This was the spirit of the official and public attitude towards France right up to the eve of the French Agreement. Public feeling responded to this official need, and went so far that we had warlike threats to France cheered by the multitude at public meetings. The situation with regard to France was changed, and very happily changed, in a moment by the Anglo-French Agreement, and I, for one, rejoice with all my heart that the relations between the two countries are so friendly and cordial. But I want to ask whether we are content to transfer the enmity exhibited in some quarters towards France to Germany, and are we content for the relations to-day between Germany and England to be similar to the relations which we brought to an end by means of the agreement with France. There is no reason to substitute enmity with Germany because we are now at peace and on terms of friendship with France, yet the fact has emerged—it is common ground to everybody in this nation—that we have been during the last summer perilously near to war. The point I desire to emphasise is that we have been so near to war without there having been any opportunity for public opinion to assert itself or to approve or to disapprove of the policy of our own country, and the policy of Germany which led us nearly to an outbreak of hostilities.

This raises the question with regard to Parliamentary control over foreign affairs. There is very much misunderstanding with regard to our demand in this matter. No one suggests that we are asking that all the delicate details of diplomacy should be conducted in public. We are agreed with those who point out that that is impossible, and, were it possible, would be absurd. What we say is that the House of Commons and the nation should be made acquainted with the broad principles which actuate our foreign policy, and should have an opportunity of criticising and of controlling those broad principles of international policy. The right hon. gentleman (Sir E. Grey) referred in a recent speech to the diplomatic barometer, and urged us not to tap it too frequently. I do not think this House at all events attempts frequently to tap the political barometer. It is not that we are anxious to tap it, but we are sometimes anxious that the Government itself should tap it, or at least should ascertain something of the broad feeling in the nation generally, and it should not only be content to be guided by the atmosphere in narrow, official and diplomatic circles. I say that for this reason. The late crisis is now a thing of the past. I think it is not unreasonable that we feel some uneasiness lest when the next matter of difference between this country and Germany arises we may have to pass through a similar crisis. All that I have desired to say in this Debate is to lead up to the expression of the hope that the policy of this nation will be so ordered that we may look forward to the adjustment of potential difficulties without the fear that any acute crisis will arise. I had the privilege of being in Berlin shortly after the Moroccan matter had led to the late crisis. I had the privilege of meeting representative men in many spheres of life and thought, and although I found most passionate feeling existing in all circles, even in circles the most consistently friendly to this country, I did not find any lack of friendship, any hatred, any enmity to this country. I rather found passionate feeling and indignation that they and their ideals should be so constantly and entirely misunderstood by this nation, and I think it is important to notice the distinction. I submit that we have made a considerable step towards a better understanding when we have realised the fact that the German nation believes itself to be misunderstood and misrepresented by this nation. One of the greatest Members of this House once described war as being a combination and concentration of all the horrors, atrocities, crimes, and sufferings of which human nature is capable. If that great statesman were describing war to-day he would have to add something to this definition, for these words were uttered some sixty years ago. To-day he would have to remind us that in a European war between two such Powers as England and Germany the cost to the victor would be as great as the cost to the vanquished, and he would have to say more than that. He would have to remind us that in the presence of such an upheaval as a European war would mean new forces would arise which would cause, whatever the result of the war, such a rearrangement of society as we have little, if any, conception of to-day. I believe myself when I consider the degradation, suffering and misery that would be brought upon the democracies of Europe by such a war that this would be the result. We must remember that to-day, with the democracies organised, and properly organised as they are, we could scarcely expect them to remain passive under such sufferings, and to bear such sufferings if they believed that they were brought upon them by the foolishness of their rulers. I say, therefore, that there would be many landmarks removed before we came to the end of the struggle.

It is when I think of the immensity of the problem and of its issues that I feel justification for rising in this House and pleading that every possible resource of statesmanship may be applied to the cause of international understandings. There are many hopeful features in the present situation. The Secretary for Foreign Affairs has reminded us that the crisis of the summer is past, and that we have a clean slate. There are other satisfactory features in the international situation. There are the frank and candid assurances of the right hon. gentleman himself that he desires this understanding with Germany, that whilst we shall be loyal to France and to our friendship with France, there is nothing in that friendship which makes friendship with Germany either undesirable or impossible. I value these assurances which come from the right hon. gentleman in his great position with so much weight, and equally do I value the spirit shown and the assurances given by the German Chancellor in his speeches to the Reichstag—speeches which were delivered under circumstances of almost unique difficulty. I am grateful for the spirit shown in those speeches. Equally hopeful is it to remember that the people of this nation are also entirely friendly in sentiment to the people of Germany as I believe the people of Germany are entirely friendly to this nation. What is now needed is surely that the forces on the side of international understanding should be developed and strengthened. Every candid, warm, and generous speech which is made by a Minister of the Crown in public is a great asset to the cause of international understanding, and every time the sensational Yellow Press of our times on both sides is restrained or its influence undermined by the spread of truth there is a great gain to the cause of international understanding. Every step that is taken to make our own policy so clear that it can be understood by our own people and by the people of Germany to be a policy not in opposition to German interests, but recognising frankly the interests of the sister nation, is a great step in the cause of international peace.  By these means, if pursued with all sincerity, we may look forward to the dawn of an ampler day when this great cloud will have receded from our view, when the concert of Europe will have become a living reality, and when, instead of contemplating European nations drawing swords against each other, they will stand firmly knit together in defence of a common faith and a common civilisation.

CANON BARNETT: AN APPRECIATION

# CANON BARNETT: AN APPRECIATION[1]

THE passing of Canon Barnett removes from our midst one who had the inspired vision of the Seer, but who also lived day by day the life of a practical social reformer ever seeking to give fuller expression to the truth for which he so strenuously fought,

"The Kingdom of Heaven is within you."

His work, much of it practical experiment based upon defined and demonstrable principles, not only secures his recognition as a great Saint, but establishes his place as a wise and constructive statesman, whose influence may be claimed as an enduring force in the life of the nation.

It is not possible within the limits of the present article to attempt any sort of history of the life and work of the Canon. The writer can only attempt to describe some aspects of his personality, particularly in connexion with the great settlement in the East End of London which stands to-day a splendid testimony to the faith and genius of its founder, who for a quarter of a century guided its destinies, and was the inspiring force in every detail of its work.

[1] Canon Samuel Augustus Barnett was born February 8, 1844, and died June 17, 1913. This article first appeared in the *Contemporary Review*, July 1913.

The foundation of Toynbee Hall, so widely and properly imitated since, was a pioneer experiment. Its conception exactly expressed the character and the ideals of the Canon. The story of its foundation has been told more than once. Here it is sufficient briefly to set forth its basic principle. Barnett believed above all things in personal responsibility. In the creation and observance of the individual ideal of duty, he saw the best, if not the only hope of progress. But ideals must be based on knowledge, and in founding Toynbee Hall, named after the gentle and devoted scholar, who had spent his all too brief life in the service of the poor, shedding the splendour of his character amidst the gloom and sorrow of the city, Barnett set out to bridge the gulf which separated the East and the West. Men, fresh from universities, which though the ancient seats of culture and research are necessarily largely divorced from the actualities of life, were to be encouraged, whilst following or preparing for the professions or the work they had mapped out for themselves, to live amidst the poor in the East End of London. Not, indeed, at the same level. It was a matter of deliberate principle that they should live their own lives, with the amenities, and the simple standards of cleanliness and efficiency, reasonably to be expected. The aim of Toynbee was never to accept a low standard of life, but to raise and to share it.

In this way, Samuel Barnett held that the cultured and the well-to-do would grow to know and to respect the poor, and to realise the conditions in a world of which they had no real knowledge. From that knowledge would spring sympathy and understanding, and the motive force for future work. It was Barnett's privilege to see his ideal realised. From its foundation there has been a constant stream of men, who for a few years have shared the common life of Toynbee and have spent some of their leisure hours in personal work in the service of their neighbours who became their friends. No one who had the faintest understanding of what Toynbee Hall stood for would ever describe it as a Mission, or associate it with the idea of patronage, or an alms-distributing centre. Nothing could be more foreign to the Canon's instincts and beliefs. He desired that the educated and the able should share their knowledge and their gifts with the unlearned and the needy; but he saw that they had not only to share but to receive, and that the people of Whitechapel had much which they could give in return. The basis of the work at Toynbee was service free from patronage and from any risk to the self-respect and the independence of those who received it. Toynbee became a centre of every form of intellectual and social activity. There were no formulas or doctrinaire views to which subscription had to be made. There was no test for entrance within its walls, save only the desire of a man to assist by his personal work the realisation of its ideals. The form of each man's work was a matter for his own decision. Classes were organised, university extension courses started; residents took part in the machinery of local Government, joining the Borough Councils and the Guardians; new social experiments were started, such as the scheme for sending poor children to the country during their summer holidays, now grown to immense proportions. Wise plans were made for the establishment of real intercourse with the people living around Toynbee. Societies of many kinds sprang into existence. Boys' Clubs were started ; organised work for the children of the elementary schools was undertaken, the young teachers of the schools were brought together for conference and social intercourse. Men eminent in all walks of life came to the Hall to lecture and to teach. Even to give a list of the activities which were maintained, would make a catalogue impossible to set forth in a short paper ; but in all that was attempted Toynbee Hall stood for the way of life as distinct from the way of machinery, realising in Barnett's own words, that the world is moved by the power which is supplied by character, by the personal influence of individuals, by *life*.

The headship of a Hall like Toynbee called for almost unique gifts in the man who held it. It was the late Warden's supreme gift to be able to draw out of every man who came to the Hall the best that was within him.

What was the secret of his extraordinary influence upon all with whom he came into touch ? It was an influence felt and responded to by the cultured and the ignorant, the powerful and the lowly, and by men of the most divergent creeds in the social, religious, and political worlds. It was not due to his appearance, for though this gave the expression of extraordinary kindliness, it was not an immediate revelation of the man.

It was not due to his eloquence, for his voice was weak, and he attempted no arts of rhetoric, though at his best there was a rich though restrained passion in his voice which aroused the sympathy and even the emotion of his hearers.

First and foremost, it was his intense sympathy. No one who came near him ever doubted that sympathy. It was instantly indicated, it revealed a magnetic personality irresistible in its attractiveness.

None of the men who arrived in Toynbee Hall for the first time are likely ever to forget their first conversation with its head. The gentle, winning way in which he received their confidence, the unaffected interest and respect he showed in hearing their views and opinions, his courteous deference, the ease with which they were led to speak of their own views and plans, but above all, the stimulating suggestiveness and the gentle counsel which ran through all that he said.

This quality of sympathy caused him to make an immediate appeal to the most widely different people, poor and rich, learned and ignorant. No man had less egoism than he, no man was freer from any sort of intellectual pride, no man ever more sincerely desired to see the interests and aptitudes of others find their full and unfettered expression. Sometimes he humorously spoke of himself as a revolutionary. To one who arrived at Toynbee Hall to serve under him in an official capacity, one of his earliest pieces of advice was not to be afraid of suggesting a revolution in the methods or nature of the work carried on. "And believe me," he added, "I am always ready to lead a revolution against myself." And he was. Convention and tradition he never allowed to hamper his work, or to stifle experiment.

But his original and resourceful mind which found expression in a thousand activities and experiments was marked by singular wisdom. Rarely, indeed, did an author of so many schemes have so little to learn from his own mistakes. He possessed an amazing judgment, and whenever he had fixed on the goal saw clearly the way to its attainment.

His wisdom was recognised by men of all parties in political life. Living a strenuous life amid the innumerable activities he had entered upon, he yet kept the statesman's outlook. The solutions of great social problems were considered by him as they arose, and sometimes long before they came into the political arena. His advice was sought and valued by political leaders, and he frequently had a direct influence in the shaping of legislation.

Many hundreds of men will retain sacred memories of the Quadrangle at Toynbee Hall. The architecture of the ivy-clad buildings which surround it gives it the appearance of monastic antiquity. To the complete stranger it is a pleasant and a surprising experience to turn from the crowded and noisy Whitechapel street and to enter this quiet and beautiful place. To the old resident at Toynbee it has other attractions. When the Canon was in residence, as he was for the greater part of the year, it was his almost invariable custom to walk in the Quad. for an hour, or half-an-hour, each afternoon. At these times his friends would walk with him, and would have the benefit of his counsel. His conversation was of quite indescribable charm, and no one left him without feeling that he had been in a rare and wonderful atmosphere.

The broadest of men, the Canon received scant recognition from his own Church. The narrow ecclesiastic and the dogmatic theologian described his work as secular, but such an attitude never impaired the sweetness of his disposition, nor did it, on the other hand, cause him to deviate by one hair's-breadth from the path he had marked out. But he had a singular power of fighting without offending. No man could have made fewer enemies.

Notwithstanding his multifarious interests, there was a singular restfulness about his life and habits. In part this reflected the happiness of his private life. But it was an essential part of his character. Noise, disorder, confusion, haste, these had no place in his nature. He was always the strong controlled character, living life at its noblest level, and illuminating all within its circle.

Who shall speak of his capacity for friendship! We can only cherish its memory with mournful gratitude and place with faltering hands this wreath upon his tomb. We mourn a hero and a leader. " My father, my father, the chariot of Israel and the horsemen thereof."

" Lead on, strong heart, lead on untiring still."

# A NEW SOCIAL EXPERIMENT

# A NEW SOCIAL EXPERIMENT[1]

A PRIVATE trust has recently been formed to carry out a new social experiment containing unusual possibilities of development, and as it is of more than personal or local interest, its aims are now described in the hope that they will receive the sympathy and co-operation of constructive reformers in the field of social reform. The founder of the trust, who desires to remain anonymous, was desirous of spending his surplus income on schemes for public good. In order to carry out his desires adequately, he asked for the help of two of his friends, and made them trustees of the sums which he hoped annually to place in their hands.

The founder of the trust considered that the assistance of trustees conferred an advantage over the method of the private distribution of such part of his income as he desired to devote to public purposes in several respects: (1) the method obtains more adequate consideration of the reforms most needed and the claims best worth promoting; (2) it secures more skilled control of the schemes when established; (3) it excites wider interest in the reforms promoted, these being the

[1] *Contemporary Review*, October 1913.

subject of thought and discussion; (4) it facilitates the promotion not only of new schemes, but of fresh developments of existing work under the care of existing societies or institutions worthy of confidence and support.

The scheme is still in its infancy, not having been in operation for fully a year; but the progress already made is of sufficient general interest to warrant some public statement being made.   It should be understood that there are no conditions of any kind imposed upon the trustees.   They are at liberty to survey the whole range of social needs, and to undertake any scheme or work they think desirable.   The trust they have under-taken involves the duty of formulating schemes, and of seeing them carried into effect, either by themselves or through the aid of other persons or societies.   From the first, however, they have desired to apply a con-siderable part of their resources to pioneer work, thus opening the way for others, and particularly public authorities, to follow.

The operations of the trustees have so far fallen into the following broad divisions :—

(1) The actual demonstration of ideas in material form.

The schemes which have been carried out, or are in course of being carried out, under this heading, include the following :—

(*a*) The organisation at a public institution of model living rooms, fitted with simple and artistic household furniture.   The assent of the Government has been obtained to this experiment being held in the Bethnal

Green Museum. Two rooms have been erected, one of which is being confined to simple old cottage furniture, easily capable of being copied; the other room is being used to show modern copies and modern original work. It is an essential part of this scheme that an attempt should be made to influence through it the homes of the people who visit the exhibition. A pamphlet is therefore being prepared explanatory of the exhibition, and giving some indication of the cost of the various items of the collections. In the same way, it is hoped to influence the various cabinet-makers in the industrial district surrounding the museum to copy the pieces exhibited, and thus to meet locally the demand which it is hoped to make for simple and beautiful furniture. The rooms will also contain other simple articles of common use, made by hand, particularly wrought-iron work, as well as examples of simple decorative pottery. An attempt is being made to obtain the co-operation of the schools in the district, and it is hoped to set a standard of simplicity and taste in the homes of those who are reached.

(*b*) The trustees have also decided to attempt to influence the beautification of city schools, and to emphasise the need for children to be reared amidst ennobling influences. They have accordingly commissioned an artist to make mural paintings which, by the permission of the London County Council, will be used for the decoration of one of their schools. The trustees are also having reproductions of other pictures prepared, which will be loaned to various schools in turn, and will be accompanied by an arrangement for descriptive essays to be written upon them by the children of the schools. One of these collections of copies consists of the works of the German artist Ludwig Richter, whose pictures of home life and of nature remain unique for the delicate beauty of their symbolism, their interpretation of child life, and their sympathy with nature in relation to human life. Each of these pictures is accompanied by a careful description, and the collection will travel from school to school, remaining at each from six to twelve months.

(*c*) Another scheme which has been decided upon is the provision of a model playground in connexion with the elementary school, with a view of showing not only how existing school grounds may be made more useful and educational by the provision of school gardens and out-door class-rooms, but also how they may be better equipped for playing games. The transformation of an existing school playground in a crowded London district is being carried out as rapidly as possible. When finished it will contain trees and flowers, possibly some garden plots for cultivation by the scholars, an open-air class-room, equipment for outdoor study, including a geography garden reproducing physical features, and equipment for games.

(*d*) The schemes so far described are related chiefly to education. Another scheme, which is intended to influence village and industrial life, is the establishment of a Guild of Handicraft in a small town, with the double object of finding work within the borders of the town for its youths and men, and of supplying the town with simple and beautiful articles of everyday use, made within the town, under conditions bringing happiness and prosperity to the workers.

(2) Research work.

Both the founder and the trustees felt that new efforts in research were necessary, for it is one of the most neglected fields of social work. They have therefore completed arrangements for what they hope is the first of many schemes for the promotion of scientific social investigation. Arrangements have been made with the London School of Economics by which a substantial sum is offered for the best monograph submitted by any student upon a question to be selected from a panel of subjects dealing with various social and economic questions.

The subjects on this panel include the following:—

A survey of the small town or village, showing existing conditions and possible improvements: (*a*) from within, (*b*) from without.

An inquiry into the economic results of old age pensions.

An analysis of national expenditure, dealing especially with the amount spent by the nation on luxury.

An inquiry into certain aspects of the land question.

It is hoped that this competition, which is open without any sort of restriction to anyone in any part of the country, will enable the trustees to get into touch with young able students of social questions, and they propose to commission further inquiries, and perhaps to make possible research work abroad.

(3) New forms of propaganda.

The propagandist work undertaken by the trustees has for the most part taken the form of grants to existing societies to carry out schemes which have been approved by the trustees. The schemes so approved include work for agricultural and land reform, including the foundation of an agricultural settlement; the improvement of local administration; educational work amongst adults; lectures and conferences on special subjects; and the holding from time to time of special exhibitions illustrating phases of social reform.

In some respects a more daring experiment contemplated has for its object the teaching of certain definite principles of beauty. So far as the great majority of the children of the nation are concerned, they receive during their school days no systematic training, or adequate guidance on matters of taste. Thus they possess no standards of criticism whereby to judge the buildings, pictures, homes, among which they will pass their lives. All the amenities of life which depend upon the observance of elementary principles of beauty are to them a sealed book. This is not a matter which affects only one social class. It affects all. This ignorance is one of the reasons why our towns are made hideous by the abominations—great as well as small—of ignorant architects. It gives us the modern buildings in Whitehall, the tawdry and unsuitable memorials erected to the illustrious dead in otherwise beautiful buildings or parks. It was responsible for the fatuous scheme, foisted upon the House of Commons a year ago, which, if it had matured, would have destroyed the loveliest park in London by running a motor highway through it. It is responsible for the patience we all display with the designers and sellers of so much of the modern furniture imposed on rich and poor alike, or with advertisers who degrade natural beauty. The list of resultant evils is without end. They may be roughly summed up in the statement that the absence of informed judgment on questions of beauty, using the word in a comprehensive sense, has resulted in a large measure in the loss of the virtues of simplicity, sympathy, and suitability on the material side of our lives, with the consequent loss on the spiritual.

The problem is not insoluble. The trustees believe that wise teaching of fundamental truths will slowly raise the national standard, and they are accordingly forming a small expert committee under whose auspices it is proposed to draw up a small book especially for the use of young people, which it is hoped may guide them to an appreciation of the beautiful in art, architecture, and craftsmanship, and give them principles on which to rest and by which to test their views. It will be carefully illustrated.

The trustees, after some experience of the opportunities before them, feel that the example of the founder of the trust is worthy of imitation among people of good will, and they propose to issue from time to time some account of the schemes they have been enabled to initiate.

# AT BRANTWOOD ON RUSKIN'S
# EIGHTIETH BIRTHDAY

# AT BRANTWOOD ON RUSKIN'S EIGHTIETH BIRTHDAY

On the eighth of February last[1] Ruskin attained his eightieth birthday, and the event was marked by the presentation of a national address, the text of which is as follows :

DEAR MASTER AND FRIEND,

The Eightieth Anniversary of your Birthday gives us the opportunity of offering our united loving greetings and heartiest congratulations.

As the representative Members of the Saint George's Guild and the Ruskin Societies of the country—owing so much of the good and joy of life to your words and work—we feel that the world is richer and happier for the lasting benefits which you have been able to confer upon all who have come under your influence.

[1] This article originally appeared in *Saint George* in April 1899 under the title "At Brantwood 8th February 1899," and the author reprints it without substantial alteration for the sake of any interest or value which this brief picture of Ruskin and his home on his eightieth birthday may have. He died a little more than eleven months later (on the 20th January 1900).

Year by year there is, in ever-widening extent, an increasing trust in your ethical, social, and art teaching, an increasing desire to realise the noble ideals you have set before mankind, in words which we feel have brought nearer to our hearts the Kingdom of God upon earth.

It is our fervent hope and prayer that the joy and peace you have beneficently brought to others may return in full measure to your own heart, filling it with the peace which comes from love of God and the knowledge of the love of your fellow-men.

It will be a great happiness to us if you will consent to your portrait being painted by your life-long friend, William Holman Hunt[1], and accept the same as the national property of the Saint George's Guild, in token of our affectionate devotion.

Appended to this our Address of Congratulation, we have the further happiness to subscribe the following additional lists of names of representatives of National and other Institutions, all of whom have directly and personally intimated their unanimous wish to be allowed the opportunity of being included in this general expression of their deepest respect, profoundest admiration, and sincerest affection.

Wishing you yet many years of peaceful rest,

We have the honour to remain,

Ever yours in faithful and dutiful service,

THE SUBSCRIBERS.

---

[1] It was impossible for this suggestion to be carried out: Ruskin was not well enough to give the necessary sittings.

The Address was promoted by the Ruskin Societies of Glasgow, Liverpool, and Birmingham, but in addition to those of the officers of these societies it bore the signatures of representatives of national institutions and of a large number of distinguished men and women in every department of public life, including nearly the whole of the members of the Royal Academy.

The decoration of the Address, which was on vellum, was done by Mr Pilley of Sheffield, and the border work included designs from the old masters.

As I was entrusted, in company with the Secretary of the Liverpool Ruskin Society, with the duty of presenting the Address to Ruskin, I venture, in response to requests, to give some account of our visit to the master.

Brantwood is a little more than three miles from the station at Coniston, and the road to it, which for the most part skirts the margin of the lake, is of extreme beauty, commanding a noble view of mountain, moor and lake.

Ruskin describes his earliest recollections of the district in *Praeterita* where he writes : " The inn at Coniston was then actually at the upper end of the lake, the road from Ambleside to the village passing just between it and the water, and the view of the long reach of lake, with its softly wooded lateral hills, had for my father a tender charm which excited the same feeling as that with which he afterward regarded the lakes of Italy.  Lowood Inn also was then little more than a country cottage, and Ambleside a rural village,

W. E.                                                    5

and the absolute peace and bliss which anyone who cared for grassy hills and for sweet waters might find at every footstep and at every turn of crag or bend of bog was totally unlike anything I ever saw or read of elsewhere."

Ruskin's house has been frequently described, and its exterior appearance at least is familiar to many. It is quaint and unpretentious, though larger than would be expected by one who had seen it from the outside only. Of the treasures within the house, through which we were guided by Mr and Mrs Arthur Severn, it is difficult to speak. They are so numerous and of such extraordinary interest. Ruskin's study is a long, comfortable, and in every way delightful room, with a superb view of the hills and lake. It is lined with books, of course—I did not see any room in which there were not some—but it contains many other objects of rare beauty and interest, including a collection of minerals and some paintings by Burne-Jones and Rossetti. Of all his treasures Ruskin probably prizes most dearly the manuscripts he possesses of several of Sir Walter Scott's novels.

Next in interest to Ruskin's study is his bedroom. It is a small room, and in one corner is a simple little wooden bedstead, entirely devoid of trimmings or ornamentation. One side of the room is covered with books. The other three are almost entirely covered with Turners, and it is these, of course, which give the chief interest to the room. There is no other room in the world which could show such a collection. Although this is the master's favourite bedroom, he has not been using it recently as owing to the severity of the weather, and the weakness naturally arising from his advanced age, it has been thought wiser for him to remain chiefly in another room, which he temporarily uses both as a sleeping and living room.

It was in this room that we were introduced to him. He was seated in an arm chair before a small table, near the window ; the sunbeams playing upon his venerable face. In his old age he presents a most impressive appearance, to which his long flowing beard adds not a little. With the exception of that beard it appeared to me that his face had undergone no material change since the days when he was a Professor at Oxford. The lines were indeed more pronounced, the expression sadder, but it was still the face which had been painted many years before, with such admirable skill, by Professor Herkomer. As to Ruskin's physical condition, it would be idle to deny that he is very weak and frail, but mentally he is quite clear, and though now unable to do any work whatever, he still takes a lively interest in the progress of the world.

When we were introduced to his presence he received us with gentle kindness. For some time it had been very doubtful whether he would be equal to the strain of receiving us personally, but on the morning of his birthday he felt better and stronger, and expressed a wish to do so. He appeared quite happy and peaceful. As I read over the terms of the address, and the signatures it contained, he listened intently and with evident emotion. When I had finished, he could only utter a few broken words, but later he dictated a further reply to Mrs Arthur Severn, and the following is an exact copy of the words which that lady took down :

"Mr Ruskin is deeply touched by the address, and finds it difficult to give expression to his feelings of gratitude, but trusts they will be made known for him. He values the address highly, and thinks it charmingly done."

Perhaps the most striking feature in Ruskin's appearance is his eyes. They are fresh as a boy's, and very bright and blue. No one who meets their glance can doubt that his mind is now perfectly clear.

We learnt at Brantwood some interesting facts respecting Ruskin's habits of recent years. Until a month or two ago he was able to get out every day when the weather was fine, sometimes taking slow walks, sometimes going in a bath-chair. In the evenings it was his custom until recently to read aloud some portion of one of Scott's novels, his love for which is so well known. He is now, for the most part, read to. *Oliver Twist* was read to him not long ago, and although familiar with it, the re-reading of the book gave him much delight. The last work which has been read to him is Mr C. E. Mathews' *Annals of Mont Blanc*.

In the closing years of his life, the master is perfectly happy. He gave expression to this fact on the morning of his birthday. He felt so happy that he wished to live on. He must have been touched beyond all words by the multitude of messages which were arriving at Brantwood from all parts of the world. Some of his friends sent poems. One of these (by Canon Rawnsley) expressed something of the national feeling. It ran :

" There was no snow on Coniston Old Man,
The Langdale lines were not grizzled grey,
It seemed the Winter had not come that way,
That endless Spring the golden age began ;
And you for whom this life's allotted span
—The four-score Summers of our mortal day—
Had dawned, you heard at Brantwood voices say
' Your springs of thought run clear as erst they ran.'
O joyous healer of dull labour's hours !
O brave revealer of dark mammon's sin !
O sure swift feeler for our people's woe !
We bring the laurel chaplet and the flowers
Such crown as angel ministers may win
To utter something of the debt we owe."

Miss Kate Greenaway sent an exquisite sketch of a group of happy, joyous, dancing children, and one of the most touching greetings I saw was from an American lady, who sent eighty white flowers, bearing the inscription :

"Eighty flower sprays for eighty pure and lovely years."

It was a fitting greeting to the great prophet in the twilight of his days, when, as his biographer so eloquently says, " the storm cloud has drifted away and there is light in the West, a mellow light of evening time, such as Turner painted in his pensive epilogue. There is more work to do, but not to-day. The plough stands in the furrow, and the labourer passes peacefully from his toil homewards."

# RUSKIN AND SCOTT

# RUSKIN AND SCOTT

THE reverence which Ruskin feels for the great master of British romancers is displayed throughout all his writings, but perhaps in no work does he give so brilliant an analysis of Scott as is to be found scattered through the pages of *Fors Clavigera*, with which book this paper is mainly concerned.

The study of Scott played an important part in Ruskin's intellectual development from his earliest years. His love for the Waverley Novels was in some measure hereditary, for his father loved them with equal enthusiasm. Ruskin has given us many beautiful and touching pictures of the simple home life of his boyish days. He relates the order of his daily life when a lad of five or six years. In the afternoons his father returned (always punctually) from his business and dined at half-past four in the front parlour, his mother sitting beside him to hear the events of the day. After that, in summer time, they were all in the garden as long as the day lasted ; tea under the white-heart cherry tree, or in winter and rough weather at six o'clock in the drawing-room—little John having his cup of milk and slice of bread-and-butter, in a little

recess, with a table in front of it, wholly sacred to himself, in which he remained in the evenings as an idol in a
niche, while his mother knitted, and his father read to
them.  These readings were mostly from the Waverley
Novels, which Ruskin tells us were still the chief
source of delight in all households caring for literature,
and he can no more recollect the time when he did not
know them, than when he did not know the Bible ;
" but," he adds, " I have still a vivid remembrance of
my father's intense expression of sorrow mixed with
scorn, as he threw down *Count Robert of Paris*, after
reading three or four pages, and knew that the life of
Scott was ended ; the scorn being a very complex and
bitter feeling in him—partly, indeed, of the book itself,
but chiefly of the wretches who were tormenting and
selling the wrecked intellect, and not a little, deep
down, of the subtle dishonesty which had essentially
caused the ruin."

Ruskin's father was a wine merchant, and though
wealthy, he preserved the old custom of doing his own
travelling.   He was in the habit of taking his wife and
young son with him when going the round of his
country customers—a journey which occupied two
months in the summer, and was performed in a post
chaise and pair.   In this way the young boy became
early familiar, not only with England and Wales, but
with great part of lowland Scotland, as far as Perth.
He tells us he used to read the *Abbot* at Kinross, and
the *Monastery* in Glen Farg, which latter he confused
with *Glendearg*, and thought that the White Lady had
as certainly lived by the streamlet in that glen of the

Ochils, as the Queen of Scots in the island of Loch Leven.

Having thus seen how great a place the works of the great writer had in his early life, we can better appreciate their influence upon Ruskin's character and imagination. Scott's novels and Pope's translation of the *Iliad* were his only reading when a child on weekdays. On Sundays, by his mother's wish, he read *Robinson Crusoe* and the *Pilgrim's Progress*. It was his mother's intention to make an evangelical clergyman of him, but as he humorously remarks, he had an evangelical aunt—and so he never became an evangelical clergyman.

Before coming to the study of Scott himself, Ruskin calls attention to the characters and lives of his ancestors from the sixteenth century downwards, and emphasises the important facts connected with each, and their relation to Walter Scott's own life. In dealing with the character of Robert Scott—the novelist's grandfather—he points out that his virtues far outnumbered his failings, and that in his absolute honesty and his contentment in the joy of country life, all the noblest roots of his grandson's character found their happy hold. He asks us to note the description of him given in the introduction to the third canto of *Marmion*.

> "Still, with vain fondness could I trace
> Anew each kind familiar face,
> That brightened at our evening fire;
> From the thatched mansion's grey-haired sire,
> Wise without learning, plain and good,
> And sprung of Scotland's gentler blood;

Whose eye in age, quick, clear, and keen,
Showed what in youth its glance had been.
Whose doom discording neighbours sought,
Content with equity unbought,
To him, the venerable priest,
Our frequent and familiar guest."

Ruskin follows this quotation by a careful exposition of its meaning and gives us one of those brilliant and delightful analyses for which he is unequalled. I cannot resist quoting one or two examples. " Note," says he, "every word of it—' The faces brightened by the evening fire,'—not a patent stove ; fancy the difference in effect on the imagination, in the dark, long nights of a Scottish winter, between the flickering shadows of firelight, and the utter gloom of a room warmed by a close stove ! "

" ' Wise without learning.'—By no means able, this Border rider, to state how many different arrangements may be made of the letters in the word Chillianwallah. He contrived to exist, and educate his grandson to come to something, without that information."

" ' Plain, and good.'—Consider the value there is in that virtue of plainness—legibility, shall we say ?— in the letters of character. A clear-printed man, readable at a glance. There are such things as illuminated letters of character also—beautifully unreadable ; but this legibility in the head of a family is greatly precious."

I must not linger any more upon Ruskin's remarks concerning Scott's forefathers, nor must I quote his description of the novelist's father whom Lockhart thought the most venerable figure he had ever set eyes on—" tall and erect, with long flowing tresses of the most silvery whiteness, and stockings rolled up over his knees, after the fashion of three generations back " —but I must turn to Scott himself.

Ruskin notes in his life three great divisions— essentially those of all men's lives, but singularly separate in his—the days of youth, of labour, and of death. Youth is the forming time. Then comes the time of labour, and lastly, the time of death. The latter, he points out, is not the time of ceasing to breathe. That is only the end of death. The time of death, though in happy lives very short, is always a *time*. He thinks that Scott's own death commences with the following entry in his diary, which reviews the life then virtually ended :

"December 18th, 1825.—What a life mine has been !—half educated, almost wholly neglected, or left to myself; stuffing my head with most nonsensical trash, and undervalued by most of my companions for a time : getting forward, and held a bold, clever fellow, contrary to the opinion of all who thought me a mere dreamer; broken-hearted for two years; my heart handsomely pieced again, but the crack will remain till my dying day. Rich and poor four or five times : once on the verge of ruin, yet opened a new source of wealth almost overflowing. Now to be broken in my pitch of pride......

Nobody in the end can lose a penny by me ; that is one comfort. Men will think pride has had a fall. Let them indulge in their own pride in thinking that my fall will make them higher, or seem so at least. I have the satisfaction to recollect that my prosperity has been of advantage to many, and to hope that some at least will forgive my transient wealth on account of the innocence of my intentions and my real wish to do good for the poor. Sad hearts, too, at Darnick, and in the cottages of Abbotsford. I have half resolved never to see the place again. How could I tread my hall with such a diminished crest? How live a poor, indebted man, where I was once the wealthy, the honoured? I was to have gone there on Saturday, in joy and prosperity, to receive my friends. My dogs will wait for me in vain. It is foolish, but the thoughts of parting from these dumb creatures have moved me more than any of the painful reflections I have put down. Poor things, I must get them kind masters! There may be yet those who, loving me, may love my dog, because it has been mine. I must end these gloomy forebodings, or I shall lose the tone of mind with which men should meet distress. I feel my dogs' feet on my knees; I hear them whining, and seeking me everywhere."

He was fifty-four on the 15th August of that year, and spoke his last words—"God bless you all,"—on the 21st September, 1832 : so ending seven years of death.

Ruskin analyses the various influences to which Scott was subjected from his infancy to his early manhood. He attaches special importance to the fact that when he was three years old he was sent from Edinburgh, where he had become a sickly child, to Sandy-Knowe. Here, Scott's grandfather, who was a true physician by diploma of nature, ordered him, whenever the day was fine, to be carried out and laid down beside the old shepherd among the crags or rocks round which he fed his sheep, with the speedy result, that the lad who in a city had probably been condemned to hopeless and helpless decrepitude, became, as he himself tells us, a healthy, high-spirited and sturdy child. Such cradle and such companionship, says Ruskin, Heaven gives its favourite children.

Ruskin tells us that we shall learn from Scott the true relations of master and servant; and that, having learnt these, there is little left for us to learn, for they embrace so much. When financial misfortune overtook him, Scott wrote :

"I have walked my last on the domains I have planted, sate the last time in the halls I have built. But death would have taken them from me if misfortune had spared them. My poor people, whom I have loved so well!" Ruskin then proceeds to quote Lockhart to show that his servants did not love him less now that he was ruined. His house was left to him and his "poor people" served him until his death —or theirs.

"The butler," says Lockhart, "instead of being the easy chief of a large establishment, was now doing half the work of the house, at probably half his former wages. Old Peter, who had been for five-and-twenty years a dignified coachman, was now ploughman-in-ordinary, only putting his horses to the carriage upon high and rare occasions ; and so on with all the rest that remained of the ancient train. And all, to my view, seemed happier than they had ever done before. Their good conduct had given every one of them a new elevation in his own mind; and yet their demeanour had gained, in place of losing, in simple humility of observance.

"All this warm and respectful solicitude must have had a preciously soothing influence on the mind of Scott, who may be said to have lived upon love. No man cared less about popular admiration and applause; but for the least chill on the affection of any near and dear to him, he had the sensitiveness of a maiden."

Ruskin bids us observe that there is not the least question about striking for wages on the part of Sir Walter's servants. The law of supply and demand is not consulted, nor are their wages determined by the great principle of competition—so rustic and absurd are they. Ruskin then touches upon modern relations between capital and labour. "No minute of your labour will be merry, till you are serving truly; that is to say, until the bond of constant relationship—service to death—is again established between your masters and you. It has been broken by their sin, but may yet be recovered by your virtue. All the best of you cling to the least remnant or shadow of it. I heard but the other day of a foreman, in a large house of business, discharged at a week's warning on account of depression in trade,—who thereupon went to one of the partners, and showed him a letter which he had received a year before, offering him a situation with an increase of his salary by more than a third; which offer he had refused without so much as telling his masters of its being made to him, that he might stay in the old house. He was a Scotchman—and I am glad to tell the story of his fidelity with that of Pepe and Tom Purdie. I know not how it may be in the south; but I know that in Scotland and the Northern border, there still remains something of the feeling which fastened the old French word "loial" among the dearest and sweetest of their familiar speech; and that there are some souls yet among them, who, alike in labour or in rest, abide in, or will depart to, the Land of the Leal."

It is not surprising to learn that his exposition of

Scott excited the warm admiration of Ruskin's readers. He was issuing *Fors* in monthly parts and his correspondents wrote " Give up your Fors altogether and let us have a life of Scott," and while we cannot now sympathise with the first part of this request, we could have heartily joined in the second. For the picture which Ruskin has given us of Scott is one which only the great master could have drawn, and I can best close this sketch by quoting from his description of the many excellences of the immortal writer :

"What good Scott has in him to do, I find no words full enough to tell. His ideal of honour in men and women is inbred, indisputable ; fresh as the air of his mountains ; firm as their rocks. His conception of purity in woman is even higher than Dante's ; his reverence for the filial relation as deep as Virgil's ; his sympathy universal ;—there is no rank or condition of men of which he has not shewn the loveliest aspect ; his code of moral principle is entirely defined, yet taught with a reserved subtlety like nature's own, so that none but the most earnest readers perceive the intention : and his opinions on all practical subjects are final ; the consummate decisions of accurate and inevitable common sense, tempered by the most graceful kindness."

# THE HAND OF THE SPOILER

# THE HAND OF THE SPOILER

London possesses few more precious things than her Parks. Few cities can offer any parallel to the beauties of the three royal parks—St James, the Green, and Hyde—situated in the heart of London and enabling its people to walk for three miles on end amid trees and grass and flowers, sometimes by the side of lakes, the haunt of rare and beautiful birds. Every year as the great city stretches itself and the area of open space available becomes comparatively smaller the value of these unique parks increases. But it is curious to see how careless both the public and the Government have been of their great possession. A few years ago it allowed a great slice to be taken from St James' Park for the purpose of making the Mall or Processional Way, as it was pretentiously described, unnecessarily wide, and the Victoria Memorial was erected. It is a memorial unsuited for the site it occupies, and it is a commentary upon the standards of taste existing that it should be considered suited for any site. The glare of the white stone is unlovely and destroys any sense of repose. The gilt angel is merely grotesque. The complete memorial is a heap of masonry, lacking impressiveness or beauty. If one stands at the bottom of the steps leading up to the base of the memorial, a solid wall, eight or nine feet high, blocks out the view. These enormous walls, quite unnecessary, are typical of the whole memorial. How infinitely preferable, instead of these walls, would have been open balustrades, not of the coarse ugly pattern so frequently seen in this country, but similar in graceful pointed design to those, for example, which are common in Venice.

The erection of this flamboyant alien, to which was sacrificed a large area of priceless grassland, had an immediate and demonstrably vicious influence. The public memory is short, and the circumstances relating to the threatened destruction of St James' Park deserve to be chronicled. Before the Victoria Memorial was unveiled a committee was considering the form a memorial to King Edward should take. It decided, as one part of the scheme, to erect a large statue of the late king in St James' Park, near to the Mall, and in place of the present adequate path which crosses the Park from Queen Anne's Gate to St James' Street to construct a little to the east of it a wide straight road passing over the lake by means of a new high stone bridge. The scheme would have entirely destroyed the unique character of St James' Park. Though really a very small park its contour and trees and careful planning prevent its whole extent being at once seen or realised and give it illusion and charm. The new main road and bridge would have destroyed all this and in place of one beautiful and mysterious park would have given us two formal open spaces, with compensation in the form of views of heaps of masonry from every corner.

The committee responsible for this most fatuous of proposals grew alarmed at the revelation of their own folly. They had supplied drawings and plans of their designs which were exhibited in the tea-room of the House of Commons. It was explained that they did not accurately represent the proposals. The bridge was shown too high, only a few trees would have to be destroyed, and so forth. The replies of the committee to the criticisms of their proposals showed an entire inability to appreciate the effect of their own scheme. They told us that the existing bridge over the water in St James' Park was ugly and that the new one would be ornamental. But the existing bridge is at least inconspicuous. It is a quaint little suspension bridge of which one is scarcely aware until right upon it. It is only a few inches from the surface of the water and it is daily crowded with happy children feeding the swans and water fowl and receiving unconsciously the best of all education.

The bridge has also another claim. From it can be obtained one of the most wonderful views in London. The question which is the most attractive view-point in London would no doubt be a matter of fierce argument. I should give my vote to the little suspension bridge in St James' Park. Standing upon it and looking to the east one sees a fairy city. Spires, towers, and domes mass together with an extraordinary effect. If there is a slight mist (not a rare occurrence in London) the illusion of a magic city in the clouds is complete.

Not a little of this effect which to be appreciated must be studied on the spot is due to the fact that the bridge is almost level with the lake and the eye travels from the water to the mysterious city above. The new high bridge would have spoilt it all.

Such was the scheme which a representative committee, composed of many worthy people, sanctioned, and proposed to carry out through H.M. Office of Works. It was stopped by action in the House of Commons. A feeble official defence was attempted. The Prime Minister was appealed to. After a brief delay he announced that the Cabinet would not assent to the scheme, and it was consigned to an unhonoured grave.

The Memorial Committee though defeated were unrepentant. A prominent peer among its members defined the principles upon which the architecture of approaches to palaces should be based. They were apparently a happy mixture of the flamboyant and the baroque.

The committee, reluctantly exiled from St James' Park, decided to attempt a partial exposition of the principles of the aesthetic peer in the Green Park, and fixed upon a site for the memorial on the Piccadilly side of the park. The Government spoke uncertainly but appeared inclined to assent provided that no opposition emerged in the House of Commons. The scheme went forward, and ultimately a model of the proposed memorial was placed in the tea-room, from whence the illustrated horrors of motor roads and bridges for St James' Park had been lately withdrawn.

It is possible that the Green Park scheme might have got through could the model have been suppressed. The entry of the model meant the exit of the scheme. It showed an enormously heavy and high building of masonry, surmounted by a Saint George and Dragon, engaged in combat according to the conventional standards imposed upon this country by our gold coinage, though, to be just, one of the errors of the latter was avoided. St George was no longer putting out his naked foot in order that the dragon might take a bite at it with the least possible trouble to himself. But we still had the conventional St George riding without bridle and stirrups. The incomparable design by the great Carpaccio might never have been painted.

Happily it was possible to deal with the model on the floor of the House. The debate on the Consolidated Fund Bill gave the necessary opportunity. It was in vain that the Junior Lord of the Treasury, representing the Office of Works in the House, assured us that all the metropolitan mayors approved of the design and that a committee consisting of 210 gentlemen representing commerce and religion had blessed it. It was apparently a composite compromise harmonising the religious and commercial views of the 210 gentlemen so far as this was possible. The measure of guilt between the two schools was never decided. One member said of it that in point of the number of artistic principles which it introduced and its strange perpendicular character it constituted an artistic tower of Babel, which would have dwarfed even the old plane trees in the Green Park, would have destroyed the feeling of an open moor which the park now gives and would have turned it into a mere site for a great piece of masonry.

The Government, having invited the opinion of the House of Commons, were bound to pay some heed to it. No one had risen to say a word in favour of the scheme. Condemnation arose in every quarter. The model was removed from the tea room with almost indecorous haste and a little later the announcement was made that the Green Park site had been abandoned.

We have written in anger of these proposals. They resemble many others which in former years have unhappily been successful. But the defeat of the schemes we have discussed may lead to lasting good if it enables the people of London to realise the destruction and vulgarisation which occur in these national possessions in the absence of ceaseless vigilance. It also becomes necessary to consider whether legislative action is not called for to give permanent protection to the parks and open spaces under the control of the Office of Works. At present the sanction of the First Commissioner is alone necessary to enable anyone to place erections in the royal parks, and it is generally only by an accident that the matter is raised by discussion in the House. The First Commissioner is under no obligation to announce such matters to Parliament. In connexion with the memorials referred to above, the present First Commissioner, Earl Beauchamp, proved himself both sympathetic and helpful, and in the House of Commons appreciation of his attitude has more than once been expressed, and of his efforts to facilitate the greater use of the royal parks by school children—notably by allowing them to bathe in the Serpentine during the summer holidays throughout the day time. In the discussion on the memorial schemes he gave a pledge to the House of Commons that whilst he could not bind his successors he would not himself assent to the erection of any further memorials or statues in the royal parks. It is therefore much to be regretted that he is apparently contemplating the erection of a great group of statuary, a copy of Rodin's Burghers of Calais, in the Victoria Tower Gardens adjoining the House of Lords. In giving his pledge the First Commissioner did indeed announce that he had accepted a gift of this statuary and reserved a free hand respecting it. It was not however understood that he was committed by acceptance of the gift to erect it in any particular spot, and it is difficult to understand why it should be erected on a spot already held by his pledge to be unsuitable for statues and other memorials. At the present moment[1] a model, presumably of the same size as the original work, is being erected in the Tower Gardens. It shows the figures of the burghers mounted on a pedestal about 20 feet high. The site occupied is a few yards from the House of Lords on the turf of the gardens. Its erection on this spot is open to grave objections :

(1) It sacrifices some of the space of this tiny but very precious lung by the river side.

[1] Nov. 15, 1913.

(2) It interferes with the harmonious view of the House of Lords from the south. The beautiful impression of the building rising from the green level which is so effectively given to all who approach the Houses of Parliament from Lambeth Bridge will be entirely destroyed.

(3) The statuary has no decorative value to justify its elevation on this huge pedestal. Its interest is mainly artistic and technical, and wherever it is placed it should not be much higher than the ground, so that it could be properly inspected.

(4) It has no historical connexion with the House of Peers, and its erection under the shadow of the Tower will remain a permanent anomaly.

There is no reason why Lord Beauchamp should exempt this statuary from the pledge he has given to Parliament. It is essentially a museum piece and could be most appropriately placed at South Kensington.

But the solution for all these difficulties is a simple legislative enactment preventing buildings of any description being erected in the royal parks and the open spaces under the control of the Office of Works without the assent of Parliament, and so giving the royal parks the protection which the London County Council gives its own parks.

When we have obtained this protection for the royal parks it will perhaps be possible to attempt to reconsider the principles upon which we are accustomed to act as a nation in the matter of memorials. At present we almost invariably choose a statue, with an occasional suburban exception in favour of an ornamental fountain. The park statue is the worst of all possible memorials. It does little if anything to perpetuate the memory of the person honoured. It sacrifices the beauty and curtails the use of the site around it. Not infrequently its unsuitability remains a permanent source of irritation to many.

As a writer in the *Times* recently stated, many of these statues scattered with such prodigal frequency suggest that they have been dropped on their way to the cemetery. They disfigure not only the royal parks but many of those under the care of local authorities. One typical example will suffice. Vauxhall Park is a tiny area in a crowded district. It is made smaller by a large memorial statue to Mr Fawcett, the Postmaster-General, and was intended to commemorate his services in extending cheap postage. In colour, design, and workmanship, it is an inferior statue. The Postmaster sits on a chair the seat of which has apparently to be supported by a pile of large tomes. An angel stands behind him. In reality she is placing a laurel wreath upon his head, but at a little distance it looks exactly as though the unfortunate Postmaster were having his hair cut. At the base of the statue there are some pictures in relief emphasising the blessings of cheap postage. One of these represents a woman who has just had a letter delivered to her. She reads it and bows her head overwhelmed with grief. To prevent this crude symbolism being lost the sculptor has chiselled upon the picture the words " Bad News."

Two ways can be mentioned which may prevent

people desiring or approving such memorials. One way seems very distant from us at present. It is the cultivation in our schools of the love of beauty, and the inculcation of a knowledge of its vital and final principles.

The other way is more immediately hopeful so far at least as the present generation is concerned. It is to point the better way. The King Edward Memorial Committee, with whose vicious proposals we have dealt, did at last adopt a form of memorial worthy of the King and of the nation. It was to turn a crowded area on the bank of the river in East London into a quiet open space of grass and trees, secured in perpetuity. The Memorial Committee at Godalming appointed to do honour to the memory of John George Phillips, the wireless operator who perished on the *Titanic*, are making a cloister, with a small garden in the midst of it, and with seats sheltered from the wind and rain. The further wall is to consist of an arcading through which there will be a view of a broad water meadow with wooded hills beyond it. Occasionally other beautiful memorial schemes have been carried out. And the choice before those who would honour the dead—illustrious or humble—is limitless. A piece of moor or meadowland may be secured and held in trust for the public use for all time ; a fragment of slumland may be converted into a healthy and beautiful spot ; a precious viewpoint may be secured by the people of a city ; trees may be planted in squalid streets ; great pictures may decorate unlovely school-rooms. Even if we confine ourselves only to the physical memorial, which is the only form properly arising for consideration within the limits of our subject, there are a thousand excellent ways in which to praise great men and our fathers that begat us, and when these are studied with sympathy and applied with understanding the formation of a memorial committee will have been robbed of the terror which it now inspires.